THIS BO

BELONGS TO

_____

This book will help you master all the capital cities in the world in a fun crossword format. The book has been separated into five geographical regions: Europe, Africa, Asia, the Americas, Australasia/Oceania. In each section the capitals are listed for learning in order of difficulty. You can then test what you have learned through the crosswords.

It is always a tough question to define what a country actually is, given the range of political systems around the world. This book has included some of the lesser known microstates that may not have full independence, but still have a high level of autonomy.

This book is accurate as of July 2020, and new states and countries are always being formed.

PRACTISE PAGE

This page will help you master the capital cities of all 51 countries in Europe. Practise these first before trying your luck at the crosswords later ... unless you think that you are already good enough.

Country	Capital city
Easy	**Easy**
Austria	Vienna
Belgium	Brussels
Croatia	Zagreb
Czech Republic	Prague
Denmark	Copenhagen
Finland	Helsinki
France	Paris
Germany	Berlin
Hungary	Budapest
Ireland	Dublin
Italy	Rome
Netherlands	Amsterdam
Norway	Oslo
Portugal	Lisbon
Russia	Moscow
Spain	Madrid
United Kingdom	London
Medium	**Medium**
Belarus	Minsk
Bosnia and Herzegovina	Sarajevo
Bulgaria	Sofia
Greece	Athens
Iceland	Reykjavik
Luxembourg	Luxembourg
Malta	Valletta
Monaco	Monaco

Country	Capital city
Poland	Warsaw
Romania	Bucharest
San Marino	San Marino
Serbia	Belgrade
Slovakia	Bratislava
Slovenia	Ljubljana
Sweden	Stockholm
Switzerland	Bern
Ukraine	Kiev
Hard	**Hard**
Åland Islands	Mariehamn
Albania	Tirana
Andorra	Andorra la Vella
Estonia	Tallinn
Faroe Islands	Torshavn
Gibraltar	Gibraltar
Guernsey	Saint Peter Port
Isle of Man	Douglas
Jersey	Saint Helier
Kosovo	Pristina
Latvia	Riga
Liechtenstein	Vaduz
Lithuania	Vilnius
Moldova	Chisinau
Montenegro	Podgorica
North Macedonia	Skopje
Svalbard	Longyearbyen

EUROPE 1

Across

2. What is the capital city of Montenegro?

3. What is the capital city of Austria?

8. What is the capital city of Romania?

9. What is the capital city of Serbia?

10. What is the capital city of the Czech Republic?

12. What is the capital city of Guernsey?

13. What is the capital city of Norway?

16. What is the capital city of Spain?

17. What is the capital city of Germany?

Down

1. What is the capital city of Jersey?

4. What is the capital city of the Åland Islands?

5. What is the capital city of Bosnia and Herzegovina?

6. What is the capital city of Malta?

7. What is the capital city of Switzerland?

11. What is the capital city of the Faroe Islands?

14. What is the capital city of Liechtenstein?

15. What is the capital city of Ireland?

EUROPE 2

Across

4. What is the capital city of Finland?
6. What is the capital city of Russia?
8. What is the capital city of Denmark?
9. What is the capital city of Gibraltar?
12. What is the capital city of Slovakia?
14. What is the capital city of Albania?
15. What is the capital city of Belarus?
16. What is the capital city the of Isle of Man?
17. What is the capital city of Kosovo?

Down

1. What is the capital city of Lithuania?
2. What is the capital city of Hungary?
3. What is the capital city of Svalbard?
5. What is the capital city of Bulgaria?
7. What is the capital city of Moldova?
10. What is the capital city of Netherlands?
11. What is the capital city of Poland?
13. What is the capital city of Ukraine?

EUROPE 3

Across

2. What is the capital city of Belgium?
4. What is the capital city of Portugal?
6. What is the capital city of Monaco?
8. What is the capital city of France?
10. What is the capital city of Andorra?
13. What is the capital city of Iceland?
14. What is the capital city of Slovenia?
16. What is the capital city of United Kingdom?
17. What is the capital city of San Marino?

Down

1. What is the capital city of Estonia?
3. What is the capital city of Sweden?
5. What is the capital city of North Macedonia?
7. What is the capital city of Latvia?
9. What is the capital city of Croatia?
11. What is the capital city of Luxembourg?
12. What is the capital city of Greece?
15. What is the capital city of Italy?

PRACTISE PAGE

This page will help you master the capital cities of all 55 countries in both north and south America. Practise these first before trying your luck at the crosswords later.

Country	Capital city
Easy	**Easy**
Argentina	Buenos Aires
Bahamas	Nassau
Brazil	Brasilia
Belize	Belmopan
Bolivia	Sucre
Canada	Ottawa
Chile	Santiago
Colombia	Bogota
Costa Rica	San Jose
Cuba	Havana
Ecuador	Quito
Jamaica	Kingston
Mexico	Mexico City
Paraguay	Asuncion
Peru	Lima
United States	Washington, D.C.
Uruguay	Montevideo
Venezuela	Caracas
Medium	**Medium**
Anguilla	The Valley
Aruba	Oranjestad
Barbados	Bridgetown
Bermuda	Hamilton
Dominica	Roseau
Dominican Republic	Santo Domingo
El Salvador	San Salvador

Country	Capital city
Falkland Islands	Stanley
Greenland	Nuuk
Grenada	Saint George's
Guatemala	Guatemala City
Haiti	Port-au-Prince
Honduras	Tegucigalpa
Nicaragua	Managua
Panama	Panama City
Puerto Rico	San Juan
Suriname	Paramaribo
Trinidad and Tobago	Port-of-Spain
Hard	**Hard**
Antigua and Barbuda	Saint John's
British Virgin Islands	Road Town
Cayman Islands	George Town
Curacao	Willemstad
French Guiana	Cayenne
Guadeloupe	Basse-Terre
Guyana	Georgetown
Martinique	Fort-de-France
Montserrat	Brades
Saint Barthelemy	Gustavia
Saint Kitts and Nevis	Basseterre
Saint Lucia	Castries
Saint Martin	Marigot
Saint Pierre and Miquelon	Saint-Pierre
Saint Vincent and the Grenadines	Kingstown
Sint Maarten	Philipsburg
South Georgia and South Sandwich Islands	King Edward Point
Turks and Caicos Islands	Cockburn Town
Virgin Islands	Charlotte Amalie

THE AMERICAS 1

Across

2. What is the capital city of Aruba?
3. What is the capital city of Greenland?
5. What is the capital city of Puerto Rico?
6. What is the capital city of the United States?
8. What is the capital city of Suriname?
11. What is the capital city of Costa Rica?
12. What is the capital city of Anguilla?
13. What is the capital city of the Virgin Islands?
15. What is the capital city of Saint Lucia?
16. What is the capital city of Dominica?

17. What is the capital city of Belize?
18. What is the capital city of Panama?
19. What is the capital city of Mexico?

Down

1. What is the capital city of Honduras?
4. What is the capital city of Saint Vincent and the Grenadines?
7. What is the capital city of El Salvador?
9. What is the capital city of the Cayman Islands?
10. What is the capital city of Guatemala?
14. What is the capital city of Brazil?

THE AMERICAS 2

Across

2. What is the capital city of Bermuda?

4. What is the capital city of Grenada?

7. What is the capital city of Trinidad and Tobago?

9. What is the capital city of Antigua and Barbuda?

11. What is the capital city of Saint Barthelemy?

12. What is the capital city of Sint Maarten?

15. What is the capital city of Uruguay?

16. What is the capital city of Saint Martin?

17. What is the capital city of the Falkland Islands?

18. What is the capital city of Jamaica?

Down

1. What is the capital city of Guyana?

3. What is the capital city of the Dominican Republic?

5. What is the capital city of the Bahamas?

6. What is the capital city of Cuba?

8. What is the capital city of the British Virgin Islands?

10. What is the capital city of Paraguay?

13. What is the capital city of Chile?

14. What is the capital city of Montserrat?

THE AMERICAS 3

Across

2. What is the capital city of Venezuela?
4. What is the capital city of the Turks and Caicos Islands?
9. What is the capital city of French Guiana?
10. What is the capital city of Peru?
12. What is the capital city of Argentina?
14. What is the capital city of Ecuador?
16. What is the capital city of Haiti?
17. What is the capital city of Guadeloupe?
18. What is the capital city of Colombia?

Down

1. What is the capital city of Saint Pierre and Miquelon?
3. What is the capital city of Barbados?
5. What is the capital city of South Georgia and South Sandwich Islands?
6. What is the capital city of Curacao?
7. What is the capital city of Martinique?
8. What is the capital city of Nicaragua?
11. What is the capital city of Saint Kitts and Nevis?
13. What is the capital city of Bolivia?
15. What is the capital city of Canada?

PRACTISE PAGE

This page will help you master the capital cities of all 51 countries in Asia. Practise these first before trying your luck at the crosswords later.

Country	Capital City
Easy	**Easy**
Afghanistan	Kabul
China	Beijing
Cambodia	Phnom Penh
India	New Delhi
Indonesia	Jakarta
Iraq	Baghdad
Israel	Jerusalem
Japan	Tokyo
Malaysia	Kuala Lumpur
North Korea	Pyongyang
Qatar	Doha
Singapore	Singapore
South Korea	Seoul
Thailand	Bangkok
Turkey	Ankara
United Arab Emirates	Abu Dhabi
Vietnam	Hanoi
Medium	**Medium**
Bangladesh	Dhaka
Cyprus	Nicosia
Hong Kong	Hong Kong
Iran	Tehran
Kazakhstan	Nursultan
Kuwait	Kuwait City
Macao	Concelho de Macau
Maldives	Male

Country	Capital City
Mongolia	Ulaanbaatar
Nepal	Kathmandu
Pakistan	Islamabad
Philippines	Manila
Saudi Arabia	Riyadh
Syria	Damascus
Taiwan	Taipei
Uzbekistan	Tashkent
Yemen	Sanaa
Hard	**Hard**
Armenia	Yerevan
Azerbaijan	Baku
Bahrain	Manama
Bhutan	Thimphu
Brunei	Bandar Seri Begawan
Burma	Nay Pyi Taw
East Timor	Dili
Georgia	Tbilisi
Jordan	Amman
Kyrgyzstan	Bishkek
Laos	Vientiane
Lebanon	Beirut
Oman	Muscat
Palestine	Ramallah
Sri Lanka	Colombo
Tajikistan	Dushanbe
Turkmenistan	Ashgabat

ASIA 1

Across

3. What is the capital city of Malaysia?
4. What is the capital city of Afghanistan?
5. What is the capital city of Laos?
11. What is the capital city of Uzbekistan
13. What is the capital city of Pakistan?
15. What is the capital city of Taiwan?
16. What is the capital city of Qatar?
17. What is the capital city of Kazakhstan

Down

1. What is the capital city of Israel?
2. What is the capital city of Brunei?
6. What is the capital city of Georgia?
7. What is the capital city of China?
8. What is the capital city of Turkey?
9. What is the capital city of Nepal?
10. What is the capital city of Indonesia?
12. What is the capital city of Bahrain?
14. What is the capital city of South Korea?

ASIA 2

Across

4. What is the capital city of Japan?

5. What is the capital city of Bangladesh?

7. What is the capital city of Iran?

8. What is the capital city of Hong Kong?

10. What is the capital city of Kuwait?

12. What is the capital city of North Korea?

13. What is the capital city of Lebanon?

15. What is the capital city of Vietnam?

16. What is the capital city of Palestine?

17. What is the capital city of Cyprus?

Down

1. What is the capital city of Sri Lanka?

2. What is the capital city of Tajikistan?

3. What is the capital city of Maldives?

6. What is the capital city of Turkmenistan?

9. What is the capital city of Burma?

11. What is the capital city of Saudi Arabia?

14. What is the capital city of Armenia?

ASIA 3

Across

6. What is the capital city of Mongolia?

11. What is the capital city of Yemen?

13. What is the capital city of Cambodia?

15. What is the capital city of the Philippines?

16. What is the capital city of Bhutan?

17. What is the capital city of Thailand?

Down

1. What is the capital city of Iraq?

2. What is the capital city of Singapore?

3. What is the capital city of United Arab Emirates?

4. What is the capital city of Macao?

5. What is the capital city of Syria?

7. What is the capital city of India?

8. What is the capital city of Kyrgyzstan?

9. What is the capital city of Azerbaijan?

10. What is the capital city of Oman?

12. What is the capital city of East Timor?

14. What is the capital city of Jordan?

PRACTISE PAGE

This page will help you master the capital cities of all 58 countries in Africa. Practise these first before trying your luck at the crosswords later.

Countries	Capital City
Easy	**Easy**
Algeria	Algiers
Angola	Luanda
Cameroon	Yaounde
Egypt	Cairo
Ethiopia	Addis Ababa
Gambia	Banjul
Ghana	Accra
Ivory Coast	Yamoussoukro
Kenya	Nairobi
Libya	Tripoli
Madagascar	Antananarivo
Morocco	Rabat
Niger	Niamey
Nigeria	Abuja
Rwanda	Kigali
Senegal	Dakar
Somalia	Mogadishu
South Africa	Pretoria
Tanzania	Dodoma
Zimbabwe	Harare
Medium	
Benin	Porto-Novo
Botswana	Gaborone
Chad	N'Djamena
Djibouti	Djibouti
Eritrea	Asmara
Gabon	Libreville
Lesotho	Maseru
Liberia	Monrovia
Malawi	Lilongwe

Countries	Capital City
Mali	Bamako
Mozambique	Maputo
Namibia	Windhoek
Republic of the Congo	Brazzaville
South Sudan	Juba
Sudan	Khartoum
Togo	Lome
Tunisia	Tunis
Uganda	Kampala
Zambia	Lusaka
Hard	
Burkina Faso	Ouagadougou
Burundi	Bujumbura
Cape Verde	Praia
Central African Republic	Bangui
Comoros	Moroni
Democratic Republic of the Congo	Kinshasa
Equatorial Guinea	Malabo
Guinea	Conakry
Guinea-Bissau	Bissau
Mauritania	Nouakchott
Mauritius	Port Louis
Mayotte	Mamoudzou
Reunion	Saint-Denis
Saint Helena, Ascension and Tristan da Cunha	Jamestown
Sao Tome and Principe	Sao Tome
Seychelles	Victoria
Sierra Leone	Freetown
Swaziland	Mbabane
Western Sahara	El Aaiun

AFRICA 1

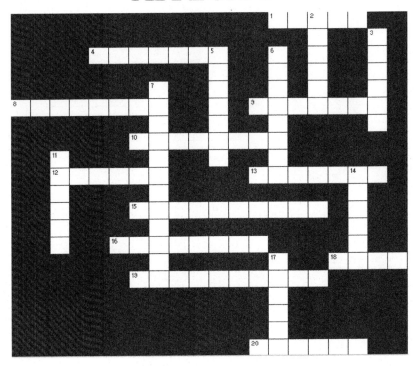

Across

1. What is the capital city of Morocco?
4. What is the capital city of Uganda
8. What is the capital city of Sierra Leone?
9. What is the capital city of Cameroon?
10. What is the capital city of Botswana?
12. What is the capital city of Eritrea?
13. What is the capital city of Sao Tome and Principe?
15. What is the capital city of Reunion?
16. What is the capital city of Djibouti?
18. What is the capital city of South Sudan?
19. What is the capital city of Mauritania?
20. What is the capital city of Zimbabwe?

Down

2. What is the capital city of Guinea-Bissau?
3. What is the capital city of Niger?
5. What is the capital city of Algeria?
6. What is the capital city of Chad?
7. What is the capital city of Madagascar?
11. What is the capital city of Gambia?
14. What is the capital city of Lesotho?
17. What is the capital city of Tanzania?

AFRICA 2

Across

3. What is the capital city of Malawi?
4. What is the capital city of Mauritius?
6. What is the capital city of Sudan?
7. What is the capital city of Senegal?
8. What is the capital city of Rwanda?
9. What is the capital city of Ethiopia?
10. What is the capital city of the Ivory Coast?
12. What is the capital city of the Western Sahara?
15. What is the capital city of Angola?
17. What is the capital city of Comoros?
18. What is the capital city of Nigeria?
19. What is the capital city of Egypt?

Down

1. What is the capital city of Liberia?
2. What is the capital city of Cape Verde?
5. What is the capital city of Burkina Faso?
11. What is the capital city of Somalia?
13. What is the capital city of Mozambique?
14. What is the capital city of Togo?
16. What is the capital city of Ghana?

AFRICA 3

Across

1. What is the capital city of Swaziland?
4. What is the capital city of Libya?
6. What is the capital city of Mali?
7. What is the capital city of Burundi?
11. What is the capital city of South Africa?
12. What is the capital city of the Republic of the Congo?
14. What is the capital city of Mayotte?
15. What is the capital city of Saint Helena, Ascension and Tristan da Cunha?
16. What is the capital city of the Seychelles?
18. What is the capital city of Equatorial Guinea?
19. What is the capital city of the Central African Republic?

Down

2. What is the capital city of Kenya?
3. What is the capital city of Zambia?
5. What is the capital city of Gabon?
8. What is the capital city of the Democratic Republic of the Congo?
9. What is the capital city of Namibia?
10. What is the capital city of Benin?
13. What is the capital city of Guinea?
17. What is the capital city of Tunisia?

PRACTISE PAGE

This page will help you master the capital cities of all 24 countries in Australasia and Oceania. Practise these first before trying your luck at the crosswords later.

Country	Capital City
Easy	**Easy**
Australia	Canberra
Fiji	Suva
Kiribati	Tarawa
New Zealand	Wellington
Papua New Guinea	Port Moresby
Tonga	Nuku'alofa
Vanuatu	Port-Vila
Medium (ish)	**Medium (ish)**
American Samoa	Pago Pago
Cook Islands	Avarua
French Polynesia	Papeete
Samoa	Apia
Tuvalu	Funafuti
Nauru	Yaren
Hard (Very hard)	**Hard (Very hard)**
Christmas Island	Flying Fish Cove
Cocos Islands	West Island
Guam	Hagatna
Marshall Islands	Majuro
New Caledonia	Noumea
Niue	Alofi
Norfolk Island	Kingston
Northern Mariana Islands	Saipan
Pitcairn Islands	Adamstown
Solomon Islands	Honiara
Wallis Fatuna	Mata-Utu

AUSTRALASIA AND OCEANIA

Across

2. What is the capital city of American Samoa?
4. What is the capital city of New Caledonia?
6. What is the capital city of Tuvalu?
9. What is the capital city of Guam?
12. What is the capital city of Australia?
13. What is the capital city of Nauru?
16. What is the capital city of Christmas Island?
17. What is the capital city of the Pitcairn Islands?
18. What is the capital city of Fiji?
21. What is the capital city of New Zealand?
22. What is the capital city of Vanuatu?
23. What is the capital city of Norfolk Island?
24. What is the capital city of the Marshall Islands?

Down

1. What is the capital city of Samoa?
3. What is the capital city of the Solomon Islands?
5. What is the capital city of the Northern Mariana Islands?
7. What is the capital city of Tonga?
8. What is the capital city of French Polynesia?
10. What is the capital city of the Cook Islands?
11. What is the capital city of the Cocos Islands?
14. What is the capital city of Papua New Guinea?
15. What is the capital city of Kiribati?
19. What is the capital city of Niue?
20. What is the capital city of Wallis and Futuna?

ANSWERS

EUROPE 1

EUROPE 2

EUROPE 3

THE AMERICAS 1

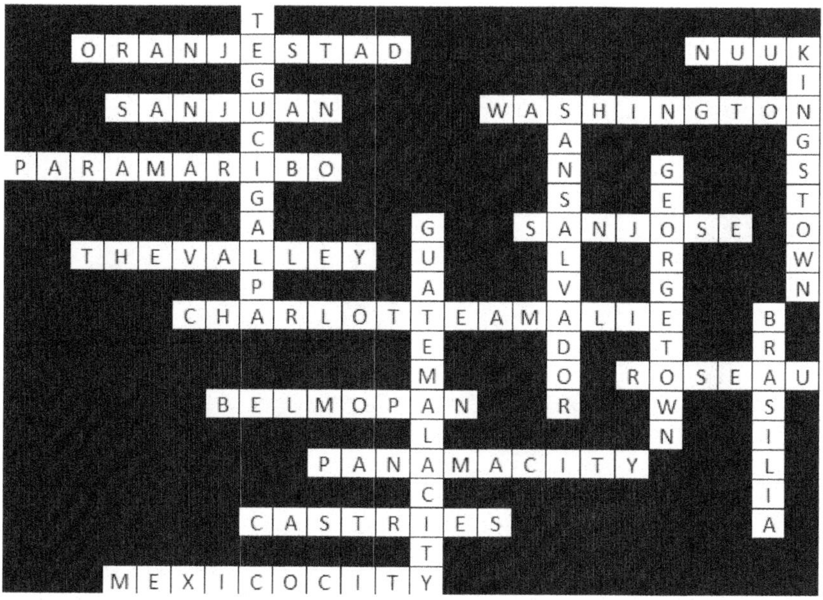

ORANJESTAD

NUUK

SANJUAN

WASHINGTON

PARAMARIBO

THEVALLEY

SANJOSE

CHARLOTTEAMALIE

ROSEAU

BELMOPAN

PANAMACITY

CASTRIES

MEXICOCITY

Down words: TEGUCIGALPA, GUATEMALACITY, SANSALVADOR, GEORGETOWN, KINGSTOWN, BRASILIA

THE AMERICAS 2

THE AMERICAS 3

ASIA 1

ASIA 2

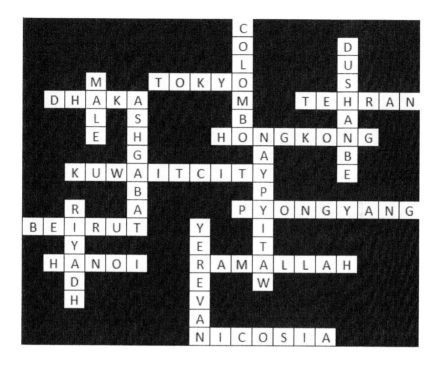

ASIA 3

AFRICA 1

AFRICA 2

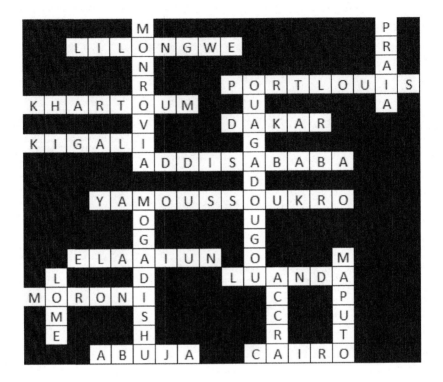

AFRICA 3

MBABANE
TRIPOLI
BAMAKO
BUJUMBURA
PRETORIA
BRAZZAVILLE
MAMOUDZOU
JAMESTOWN
VICTORIA
MALABO
BANGUI

LUSAKA
KINSHASA
WINDHOEK
LIBREVILLE
PORTNOVO
CONAKRY
TUNIS

AUSTRALASIA AND OCEANIA

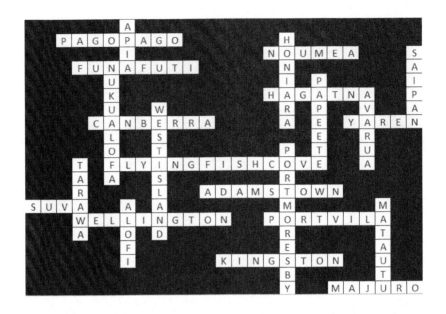

Printed in Great Britain
by Amazon